GW01376939

GUITAR

The Guitar Book for Kids

Sebastian Schulz, emusika publishing

About this book

Have fun becoming a guitar player.
I am so excited that you want to learn how to play the guitar with me. I am going to show you some awesome songs and pretty soon we will have so much fun playing the guitar together.

Your Felix

But first, some information for your parents:

This book is divided into levels that build up on each other. Your child will complete each level one after the other. Every level requires approx. 1 – 2 months of practice. Of course some lessons could be faster while others might take longer. That's totally fine, because every child is supposed to be able to have fun and learn playing this instrument at their own pace.
The way the lessons are designed, your child is not only learning single guitar chords and tones. After he or she has completed all lessons in the book, your child will know several different playing methods and techniques. During the first lessons we deliberately did not list the guitar notes, so that the kids can concentrate on the technique alone. In addition, every song features a video tutorial, which helps with the successful completion of each lesson. It almost feels like having a guitar teacher right there with you. We wish you much fun and success with the most beautiful hobby in the world
- playing the guitar.

The Comprehensive Guitar Guide for Kids

The Comprehensive Guitar Guide for Kids.Learning to play the guitar with songs for children | Including great-sounding audio files for guitar accompaniment and sing along | Playing guitar made simple with child appropriate guitar lessons.

This Book Belongs:

____

IMPRESSUM

Publisher: emusika UG (haftungsbeschränkt)
Author: Sebastian Schulz
Cover Design,Illustration: Sebastian Schulz
Proofreading: emusika Verlag
Other Contributors: Björn Horstmann
Edition: 1

Publisher: emusika Verlag, Hannover
ISBN 979-8-6794938-2-7

Table of Contents

LEVEL 1

Basic Chords

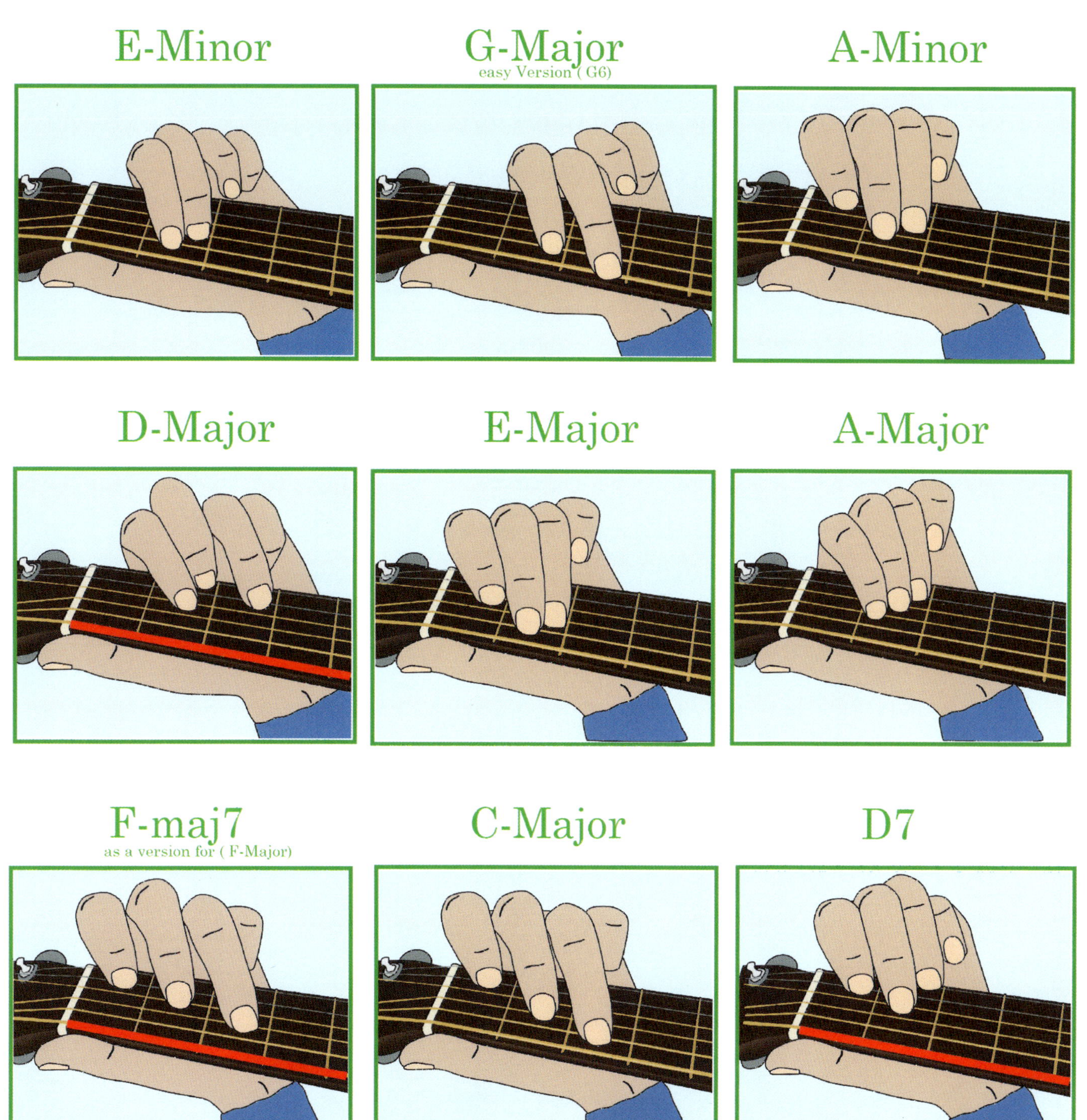

On this page you will find the chords that are most important for us. Try to memorize them over time. This will help you accompany songs with the guitar later.

The Parts of a Guitar

Before we start playing, we will take a closer look at the guitar itself.
Get to know its parts better, because later on in the book you will meet many of them again.

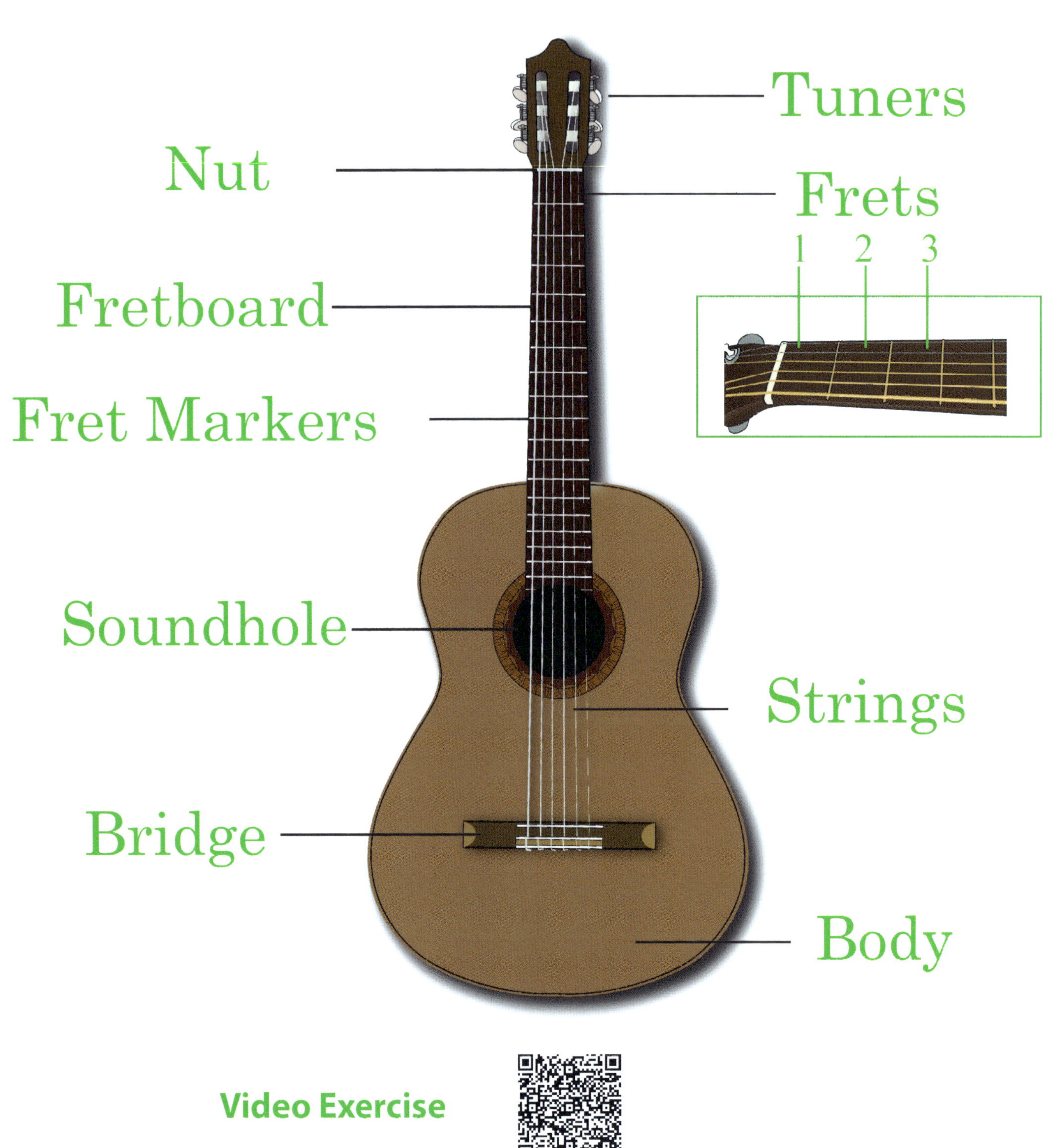

Video Exercise

Guitar Posture

Right

or

If you want to learn how to play the guitar really well, you need great guitar posture. Take a good look at the pictures and sit down exactly as shown on one of the two top pictures.

Wrong

Those three pictures are showing you how not to sit. When you sit this way, it is impossible to play the chords and notes correctly and also, after some time, your back is likely going to hurt.

The Strings

A guitar has 6 strings. These strings are of different thicknesses and they all produce a different sound.

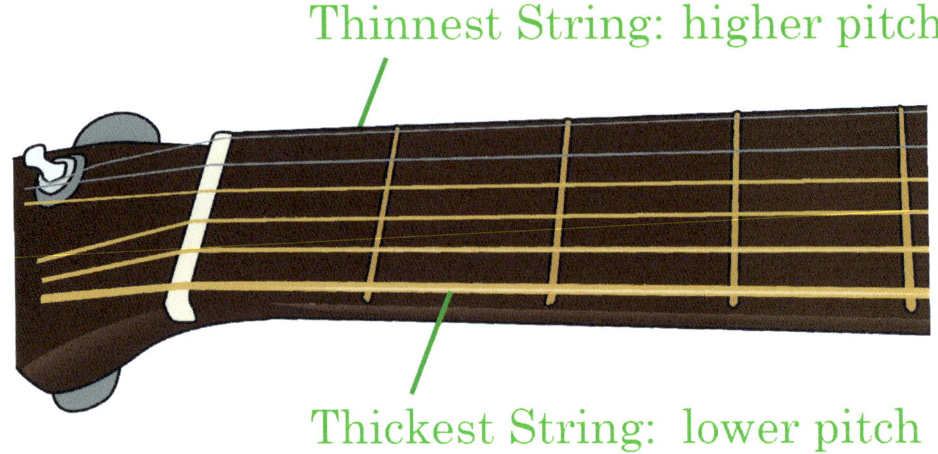

All 6 strings also have their own name, or to be exact, their own note.

Try to learn the names of the strings on your guitar.

Here is a helpful phrase that will help you remember the names:

Elephants - And - Donkeys - Grow - Big - Ears

Thickest String--Thinnest String

Tuning the guitar

Before we can start playing the guitar, we actually have to tune it first. The best way to do that is by using a guitar tuner. The so-called clip-on tuner, which is a tuner that has to be attached to the guitar, measures the vibrations when a string is plucked. It then shows you, if the tone produced by the string hits the right note or not.

Clip-Tuner

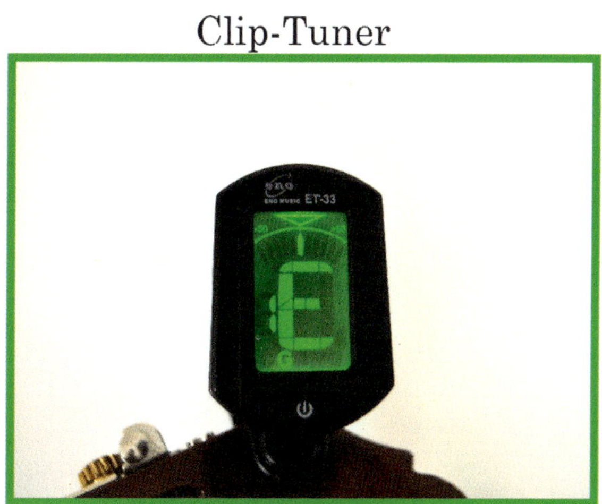

After attaching the tuner, pluck the low E-string. The vibrations will move the needle on the tuner. If the needle stops exactly in the middle and the display shows you a green E, then the string is perfectly tuned.

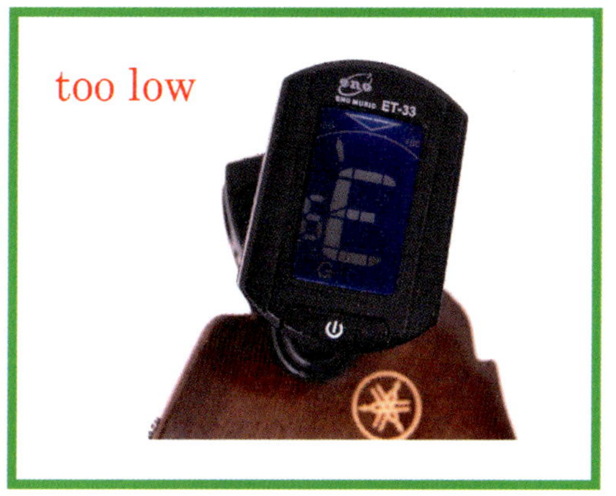

If the needle stops too far to the left, then the pitch produced by the string is too low. Now you have to turn the tuning peg of the guitar string away from you. If the needle stopped too far to the right, the string's pitch is too high and you have to tune lower, which means turn the peg towards you. Continue to tune all other strings the same way.

The First Chord

It is time to learn our first chord. It is called E-minor.

Place your index finger on the 2. string (from the top) in the second fret. Next, put your middle finger on the third string, also in the second fret.

E-minor

Video Exercise

Your thumb rests on the back of the guitar neck. Push your index and middle finger down on the fingerboard. Make sure that your other fingers (ring finger and pinkie) do not touch the fingerboard.

There is our first chord: E-minor.

With the thumb of your right hand you will now strum all of the strings from thickest to thinnest, one after the other.

The Chord G-Major

Video Exercise

E-Minor

Awesome, you have already learned your first chord, E-minor. For your second chord pick up that middle finger and place it on the third fret on the low E-string. Your index finger remains in the second fret of the A-string. This second chord is called G-major.

G-Major

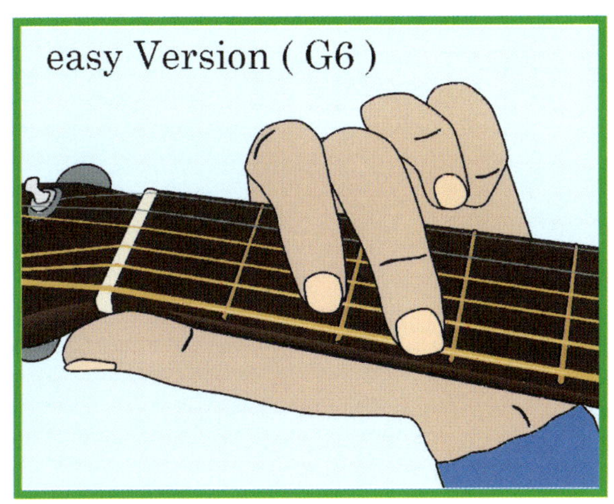

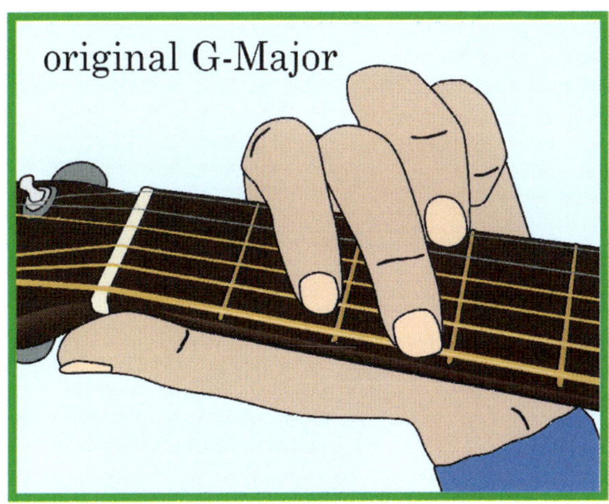

At first, you may play this chord without your ring finger, because the placement of the ring finger can be a little bit difficult in the beginning. When you get used to this new chord, you can add it in later. So once you feel comfortable, place it on the high e-String in the third fret.

Our First Strumming Pattern

Thumb

Playalong Song

Play the chord E-minor 4 times back-to-back. With every strum, count in your head (1...2...3...4)
Once you get to 4 start over again.
We actually just played our first pattern.

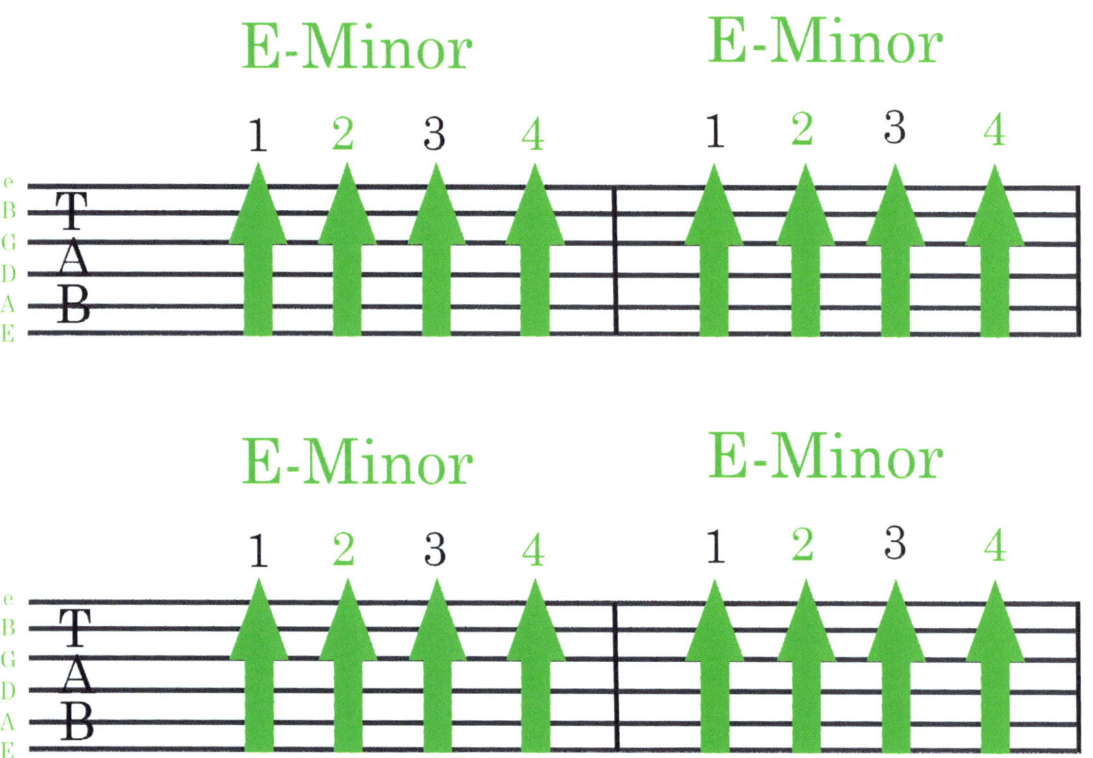

Changing Chords

Video Exercise

E-Minor

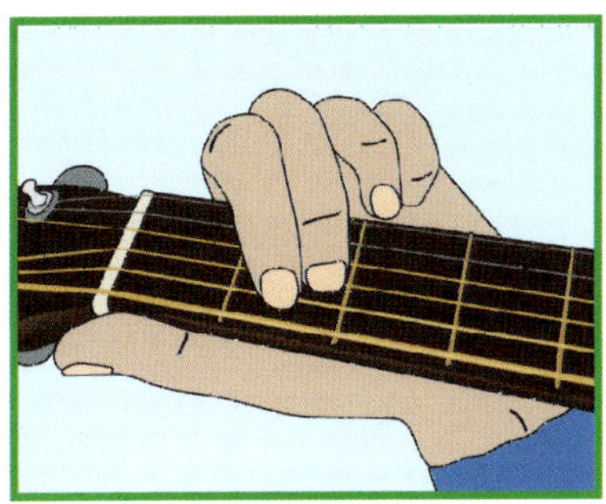

G-Major

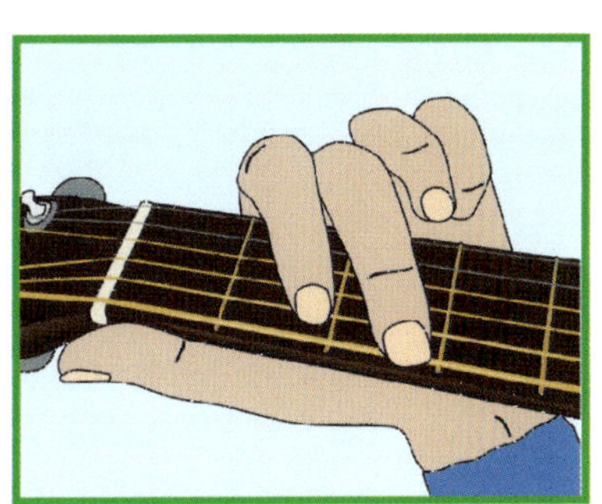

We will now try to switch the chord from E-minor to G-major. First, play the E-Minor chord four times. Then change the placement of your fingers and play the G-major chord another four times, before starting over again.

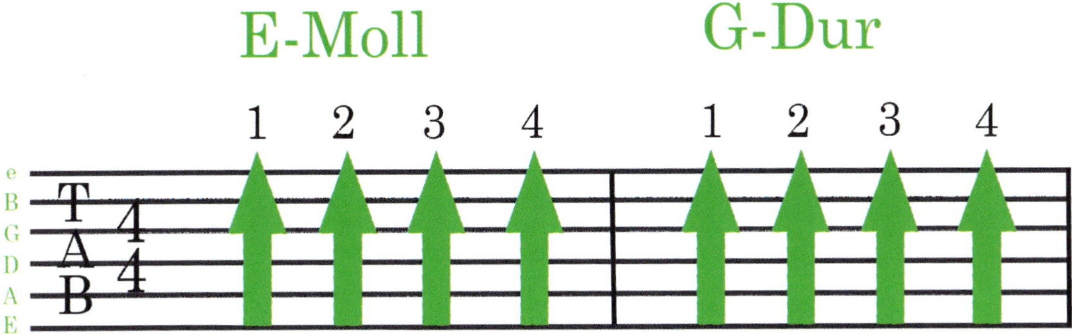

Try to repeat this change several times, until your fingers are comfortable switching from E-minor to G-major. That sounds pretty good to start off, right? Now, after some practice, we can move on to our first song…

Why does it not sound right ?

Especially during the first days and months it is possible that there will be certain notes and chords that just do not want to sound right. Maybe you can hear a slight scratching when you play the string, which makes the chord not sound so nice. The cause may be that you are not reaching far enough into the right of the fret.

The more you are reaching into the right of the fret, the better your tone will sound. Besides, that means you will need less energy.

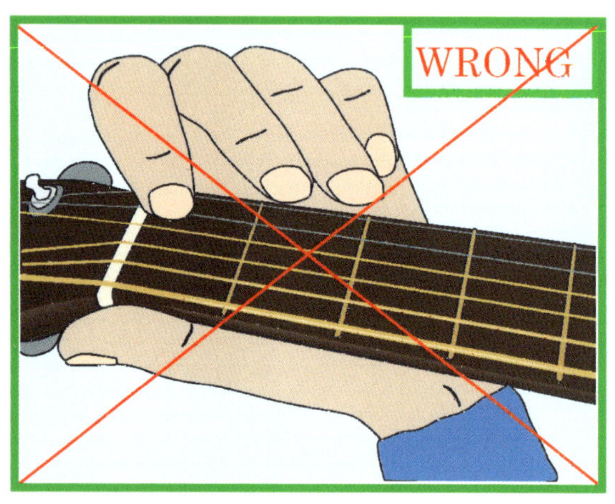

But be careful, it is important that you don't place your fingers directly on the fret ridge by accident. This would make the tone sound dull and a little bit off.

The same applies to chords by the way.

Video Exercise

Are You Sleeping ? (Brother John)

Beat: 4/4

Video Exercise

For your very first song "Brother John" we will now need the chord G-major. You probably know the song, so that you can sing along while you play the guitar. Whenever you pass a light-colored word, you play the chord G-major that is written above the text.

G-Major G-Major G-Major G-Major G-Major G-Major
Are you Slee - ping ? Are you Slee - ping ? Bro - ther John!

G-Major G-Major G-Major G-Major
Bro - ther John! Morning bells are ring - ing !

G-Major G-Major G-Major G-Major G-Major G-Major
Morning bells are ring - ing ! Ding, dang dong! Ding, dang, dong!

G-Major (or G6)

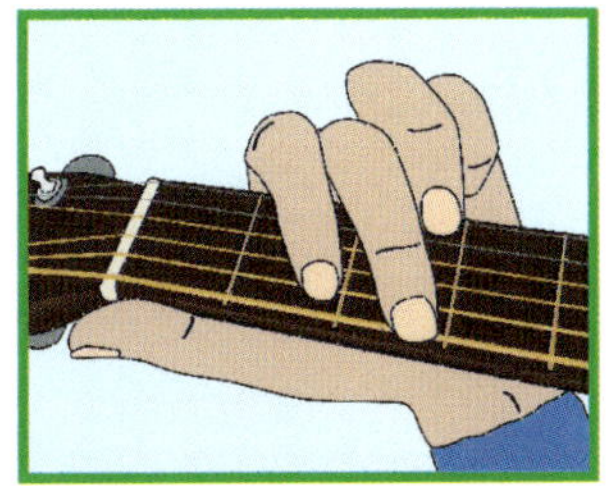

Playalong Song

D-Major and A-Major Chords

D-Major

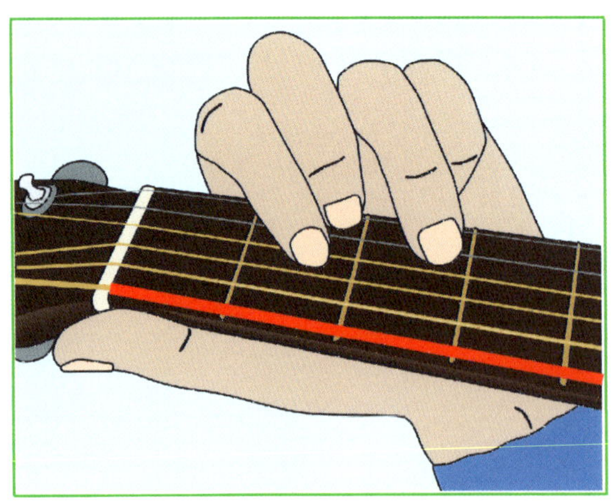

do not play the low E-string

When playing the D-major chord make sure not to play the low E-string again. This phrase will help you remember:

> D with E we don`t wanna see

A-Major

Your next chord is A-major. With this chord all of your fingers are placed very close together. It is important that all of your fingers are actually located in the second fret.

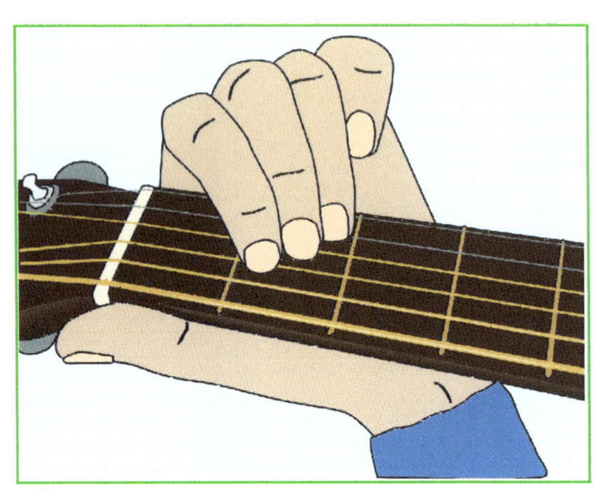

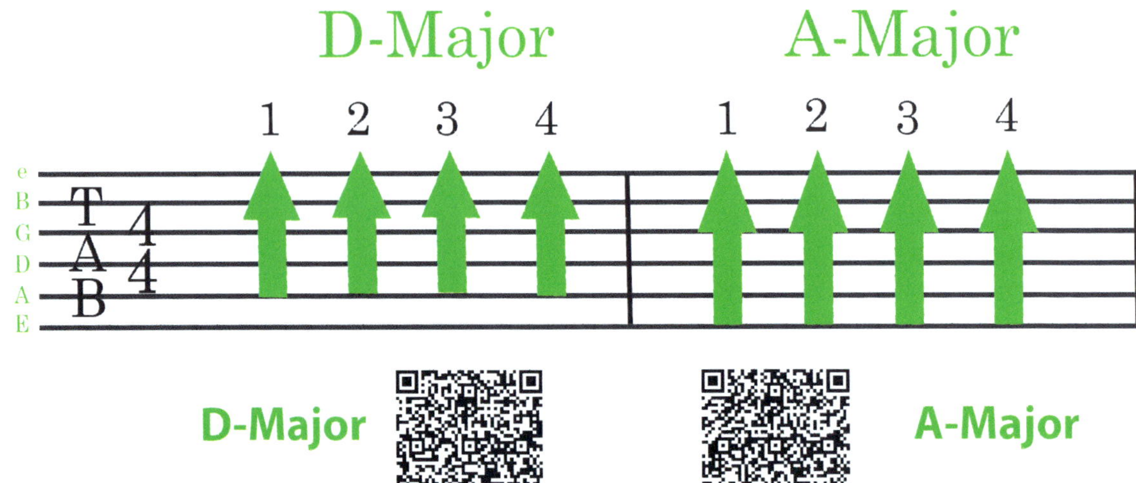

D-Major

A-Major

Happy Birthday to you

Measure: 3/4 Music: Traditional

Now that you already know how to play four chords, you are ready for the next song. For „Happy Birthday" we will need to play the chords D-major, A-major and G-major. Whenever you pass a light-colored word you play the chord 1x that is written above the text.

english

D-Major A-Major A-Major D-Major
Hap - py birth - day to you! Hap - py birth - day to you

D-Major G-Major D-Major A-Major D-Major
Hap - py birth - day dear *NA-ME*. Hap - py birth - day to you.

spanish

D-Major A-Major A-Major D-Major
Cumple - años fe - liz! Cumple - años fe - liz! te de-

D-Major G-Major D-Major A-Major D-Major
se - amos *to -do*, Cumple - años fe - liz!

D-Major

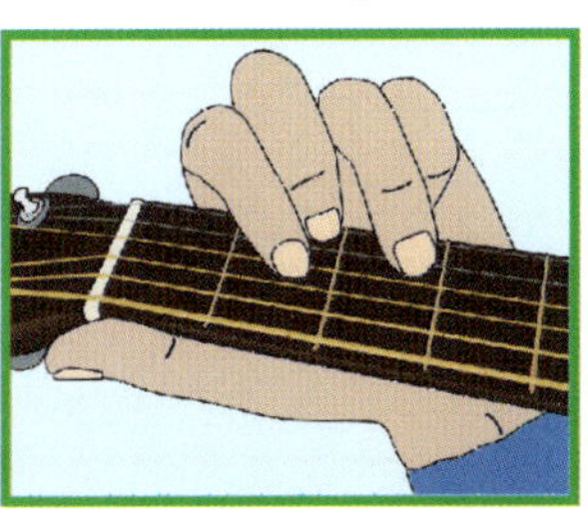

A-Major

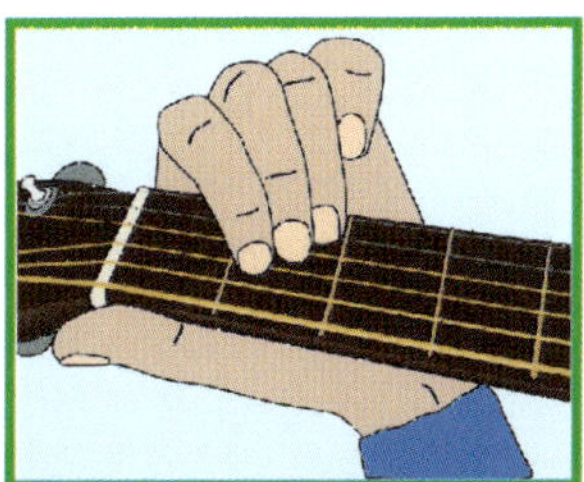

G-Major (or G6)

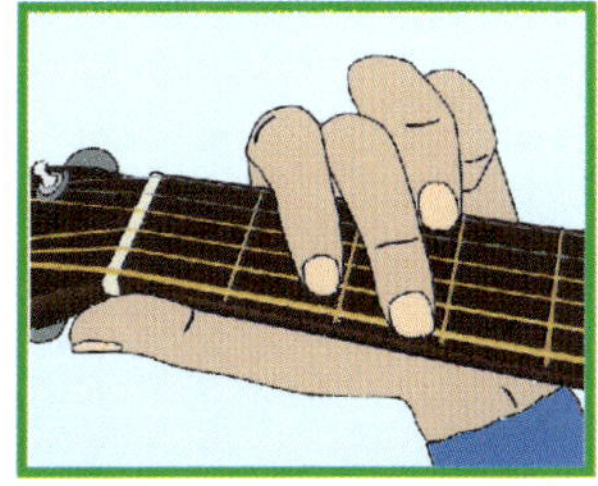

Playalong Song slow

Playalong Song faster

If your happy and you know it

Measure: 4/4

Music: Traditional
Vocals: Traditional

Verse 1

D-Major A-Major
If you're hap - py and you know it clap your hands.

A-Major D-Major
If you're hap - py and you know it clap your hands.

G-Major G-Major
If you' re hap - py and you know it and you

D-Major D-Major
real - ly want to show it

D-Major A-Major
If you're hap - py and you know it clap your hands.

Playalong Song

Verse 1

D-Major A-Major
If you're hap - py and you know it stomp your feet.

A-Major D-Major
If you're hap - py and you know it stomp your feet.

G-Major G-Major
If you' re hap - py and you know it and you

D-Major D-Major
real - ly want to show it

D-Major A-Major
If you're hap - py and you know it stomp your feet.

Video

In Conclusion / Questions

Name the different parts of the guitar

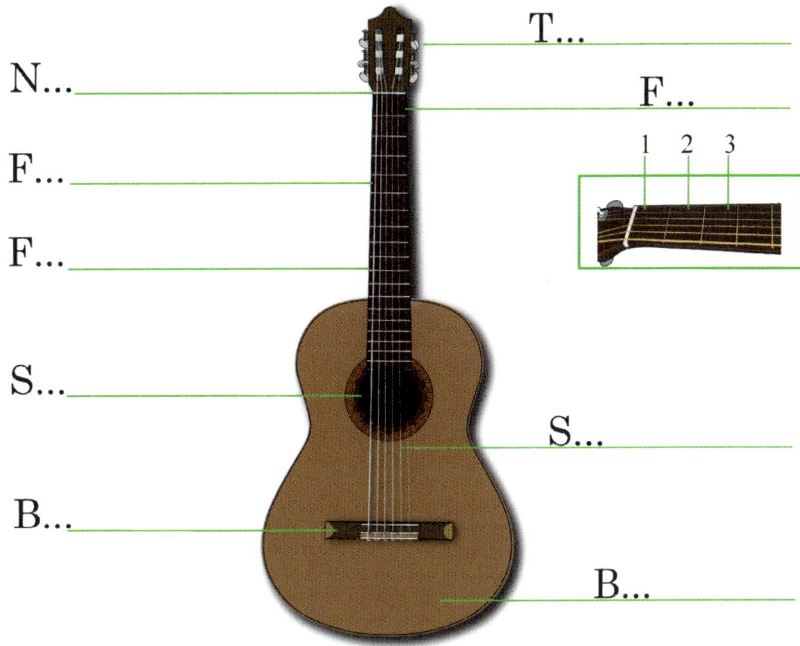

What are the names of the guitar strings?

Name two chords that you have already learned!

What do you have to play close attention to when playing

LEVEL 2

The Tabulature

Tablature allows us to play songs on the guitar, even without knowing how to read music. The tablature diagrams consist of six lines, that stand for the strings of the guitar.

The top line symbolizes the high e-string (the thinnest string of your guitar) and the bottom line is the low E-string (the thickest string of your guitar).

Furthermore, the lines of the tablature diagram are marked with numbers. Those lines are supposed to show you in which fret your fingers must be put and played. (In our example we are placing our finger on the B-string in the second fret)

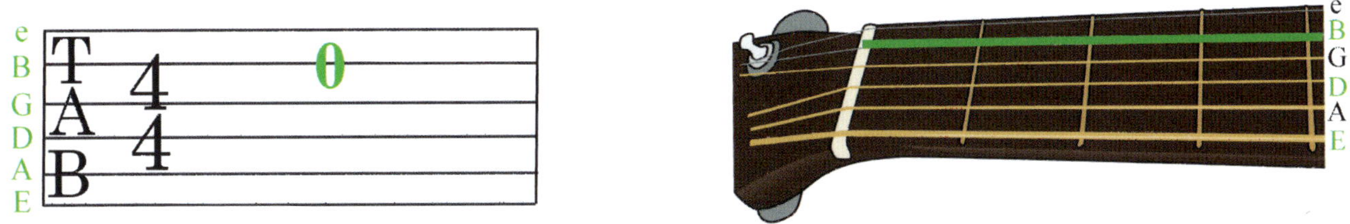

If the tablature shows a „0“ then that means that you have to play the string without finger placement.

Tablature Exercises

During the following exercises we are playing the strings with our right hand thumb. This means we have to pluck the string without touching any of the other ones.

Our first tablature exercise lists a "0" on the third string from the bottom. This is the D-string. The D-string is played 4x per tact during this exercise.

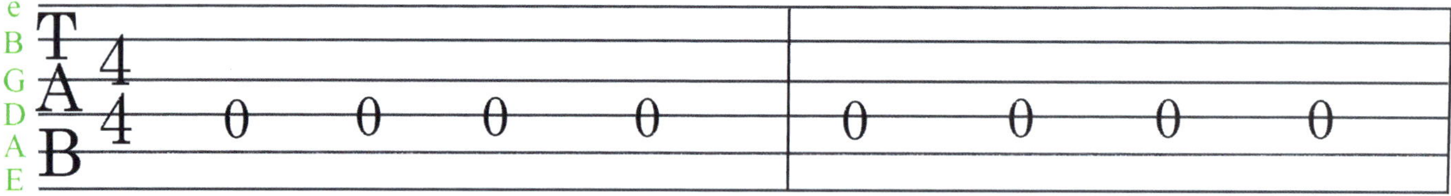

In the next exercise we are going to switch back and forth between two strings. Let's start with the D-string again. Play it first and then play the G-string after.

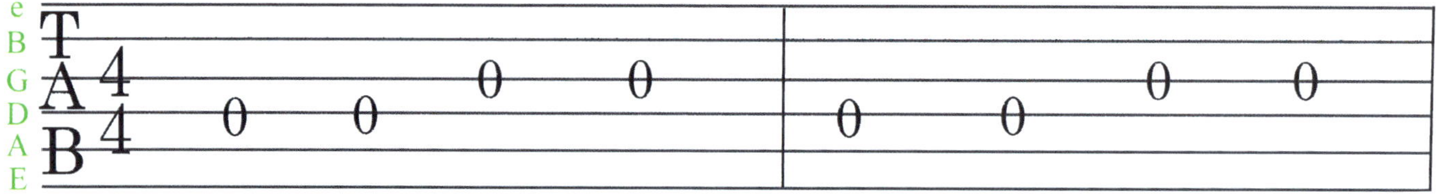

If you can manage not to play another string by accident, you are ready for the exercises on the next page.

Video Exercise

Tablature Extended

Now we are going to add additional fingers on the fretboard. First, play the open (0) D-string again, then place a finger in the second fret and after that, another one in the third fret.

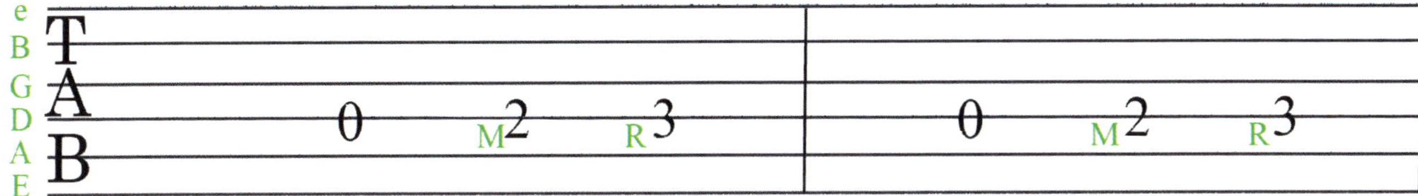

The little letters next to the numbers indicate, which finger of your left hand is fretting the note.
These are the abbreviations:

I = Index Finger
M= Middle Finger
R = Ring Finger
P = Pinkie Finger

Next we want to play across several strings. Start on the A-string in the 3rd fret and slowly play the notes one after the other up to the empty G-string.

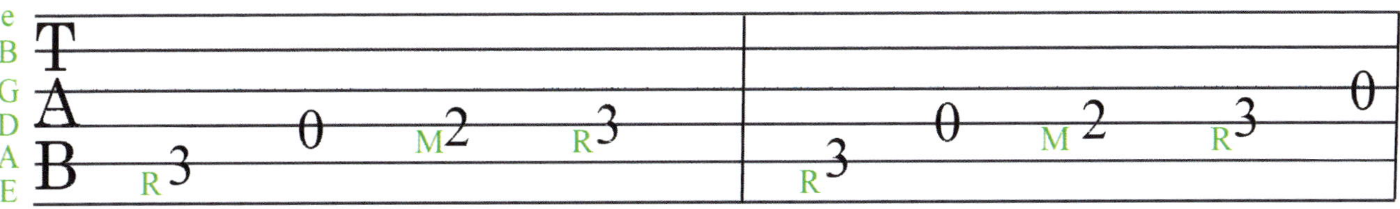

Video Exercise

Finger Gymnastics

With the next exercise we want to continue practicing with our fingers. You will do this by playing your first scale:

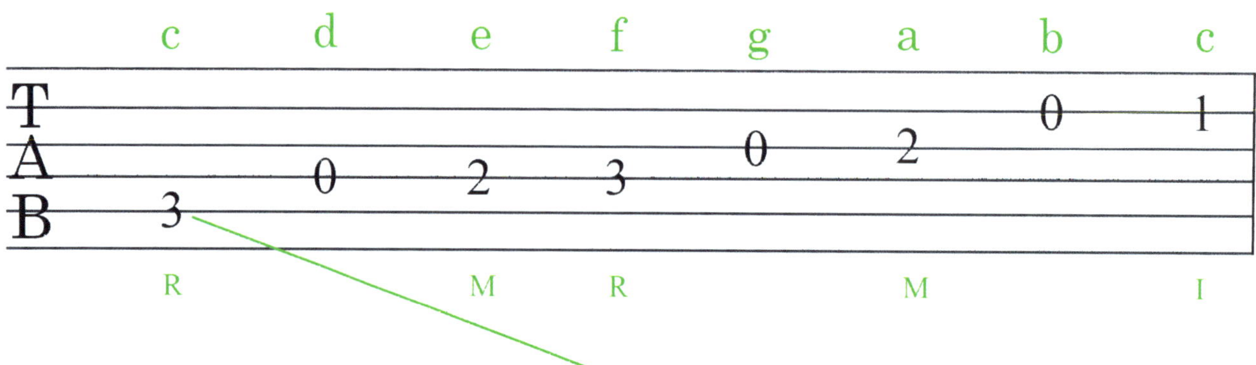

Start off by placing your ring finger in the 3rd fret.

Important! Play each note with the corresponding finger and after you have learned how to play the scale forward, try playing it backwards.

c b a g f e d c

T
A
B

1 0 2 0 3 2 0 3

I M R M R

Playalong Song slow

Playalong faster

The Guitar Sprint

By now you probably already know the C-major scale by heart. Now let's see how fast you can play it. Ask mom, dad or another family member to time you.

You are now playing from low C to high c.

Every note should be played neatly and correctly.
If you make a mistake, you just start all over again.

1 ______________ seconds

2 ______________ seconds

3 ______________ seconds

4 ______________ seconds

5 ______________ seconds

6 ______________ seconds

7 ______________ seconds

8 ______________ seconds

9 ______________ seconds

10 ______________ seconds

Your best time:

______________ seconds

Oh when the saints

Video

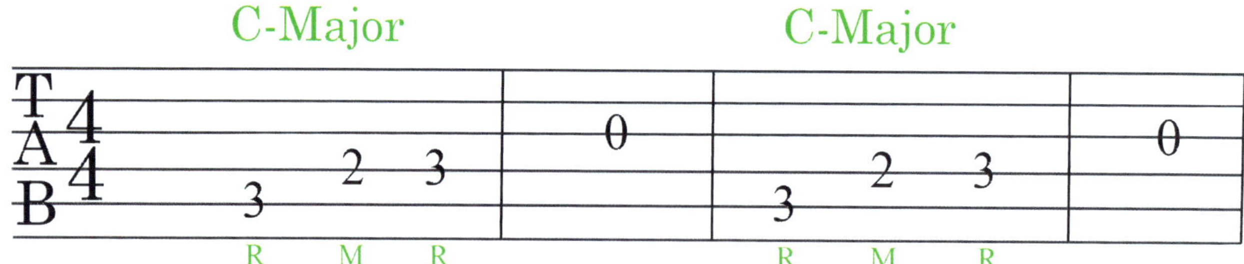

C-Major C-Major G-Major

TAB 4/4

3 2 3	0 2	3 2	0
R M R	M	R M	

C-Major F-Major

TAB 4/4

2 2 0	3 3	2 0	0 3
M M	R R	M	R

C-Major G-Major C-Major

TAB 4/4

2 3	0 2	0 0	3
M R	M		R

Playalong Song

Row, Row, Row your boat

Video

C-Major C-Major

T
A
B

2 3 0 1 1 1 0 0 0

M R I I I

C-Major G-Major

T
A
B

2 2 2 3 3 3 0 3

M M M R R R R

G-Major C-Major

T
A
B

2 0 3

M R

LEVEL 3

Our Next Chords

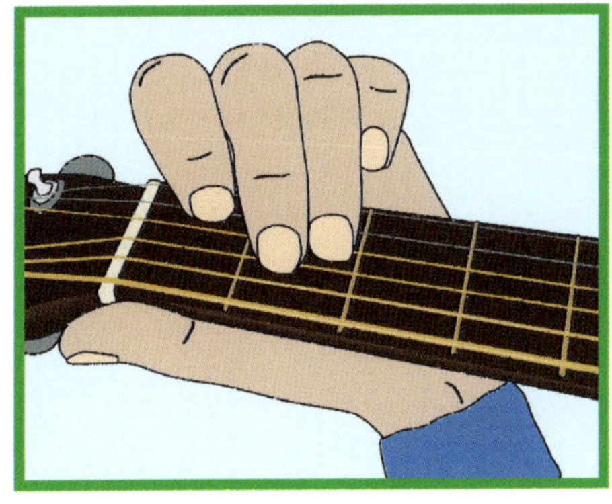

Video Exercise

A-Minor

In order to play the chord A-minor we will need to use the three fingers of our left hand again (index, middle and ring finger). Be careful not to touch the high e-string with the palm of your hand.

Your next chord is called D-7. When playing this chord, you must avoid the low E-string. Now try to change chords from A-minor to D7. Remember not to play the low E-string!

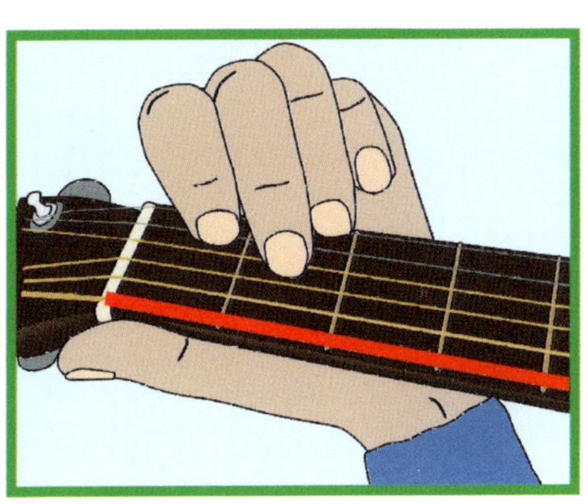

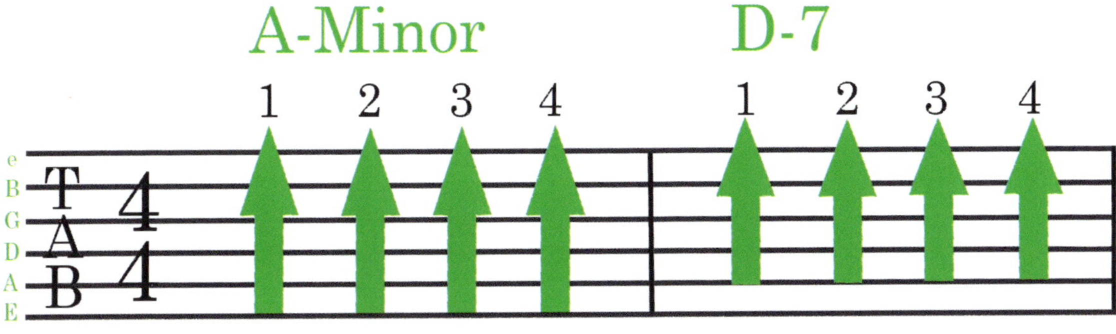

Playalong Song slow

Playalong Song faster

Chord Workout

Next, we are going to play a sequence of four chords. This will help us practice our chord-changing technique.

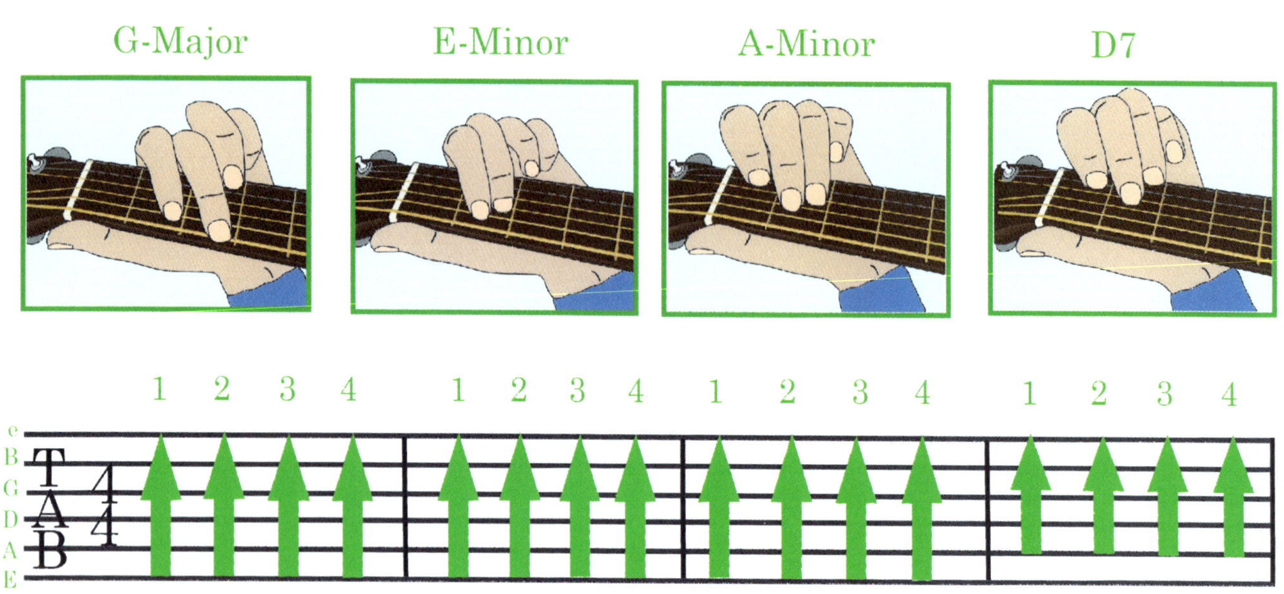

Did everything work out well? Great! Now you are ready for your next song. If you want, you can still play the „simple G-Major" right now.

Our next song is called: "I love the mountains". The chord change is the same as in the example above: G-e-a-D7. Every time you get to a light-colored word, you have to play the chord.

Additionally, you will see that there are notes. Those are the vocal melody. At this point however, the only thing that is important to us are the chords above the notes.

Video Exercise

I love the mountains

Melody/Vocals: Traditional

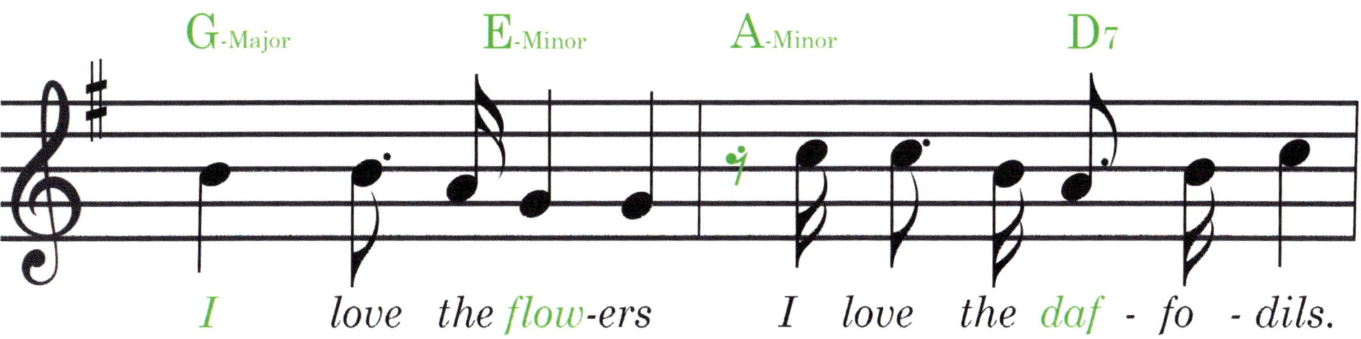

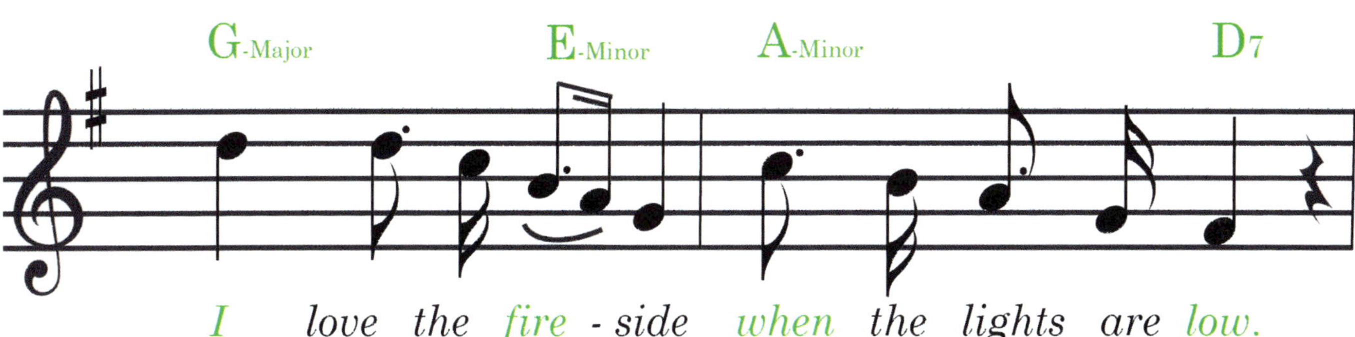

Playalong Song
faster

Alternate Picking (Picado)

Up until now we have played all notes with the thumb of the right hand. But there is also another technique that allows us to play faster paced melodies. This method is called Alternate Picking.

When practicing Alternate Picking we switch back and forth between using the middle (m) and index finger (i) to play the corresponding string. Meanwhile the thumb stays on the low E-string.

```
    m  i  m  i   |  m  i  m  i   |  m  i  m  i
 -- 0--0--0--0---|--0--0--0--0---|--0--0--0--0---|
T ---------------|---------------|---------------|
A ---------------|---------------|---------------|
B ---------------|---------------|---------------|

    m  i  m  i   |  m  i  m  i   |  m  i  m  i
 ----------------|---------------|---------------||
T --0--0--0--0---|--0--0--0--0---|--0--0--0--0--o||
A ---------------|---------------|--------------o||
B ---------------|---------------|---------------||
```

Video Exercise

Flamingo Flamenco

Video Exercise

During our next exercise, called the „Flamingo Flamenco“, we are going to practice the Alternate Picking technique. Above the notes, in light-colored letters, you can read which finger of the left hand to use to play.

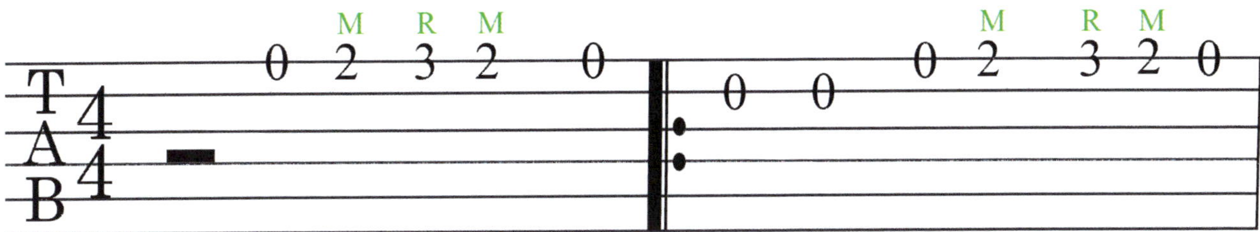

M M M R M I I I R R I
2 2 0 2 3 2 0 1 1 1 3 0 3 1
TAB

1. 2.
M R M
0 0 2 3 2 0 0
TAB

Additionally, there are two brackets. Together with the repeat mark they mean that in the first round you play bracket one until the end, then circle back to tact 2 and this time play bracket two right away. (Meaning skipping tact 5).

Playalong Song slow

Playalong Song faster

Itsy Bitsy Spider

Video

Play the song with our Alternate picking technique (Picado)

```
                 G-Major                            D-Major
  |-------------|-----------------|-----------|---------------|
T |-------------|-----------------|-0---0---0-|------------0--|
A 6-------------|-0----0----2-----|-----------|-2--0---2------|
B 8-----0-------|-----------------|-----------|---------------|
  |-------------|-----------------|-----------|---------------|
  |-------------|-----------------|-----------|---------------|
                            M                   M      M
```

```
        G-Major                               D-Major          G-Major
  |----------|---------------|---------|-----------------|--------|
T |----------|-0----0----1---|-3----3--|-1---0---1---3---|---0----|
A |----0-----|---------------|---------|-----------------|--------|
  |----------|---------------|---------|-----------------|--------|
B |----------|---------------|---------|-----------------|--------|
  |----------|---------------|---------|-----------------|--------|
                         I     R    R    I       I   R
```

```
        G-Major                      D-Major                G-Major
  |-----------------|----------|--------------------|-----------|
T |-----------------|-0----0---|-----------------0--|-----------|
A |--0----0----2----|----------|-2---0----2---------|-0---------|
  |-----------------|----------|--------------------|------0--0-|
B |-----------------|----------|--------------------|-----------|
  |-----------------|----------|--------------------|-----------|
               M                 M        M
```

```
        G-Major                          D-Major          G-Major
  |----------------------|----------|---------------------------|
T |----------------------|-0----0---|-----------------0---------|
A |--0---0---0---2-------|----------|-2----0----2-----------0---|
  |----------------------|----------|---------------------------|
B |----------------------|----------|---------------------------|
  |----------------------|----------|---------------------------|
                 M                    M          M
```

Playalong Song

E-Major Chord

The next chord is already waiting for you.

E-major's finger placement is very similar to A-minor. For E-major all fingers are simply sliding up by one string.

E-Major

Video Exercise

Changing Chords

This new chord is going to help us practice our chord changes. Play every chord twice before switching over to a new one. Practice the chord change until you start feeling confident about it.

2x

D-Major

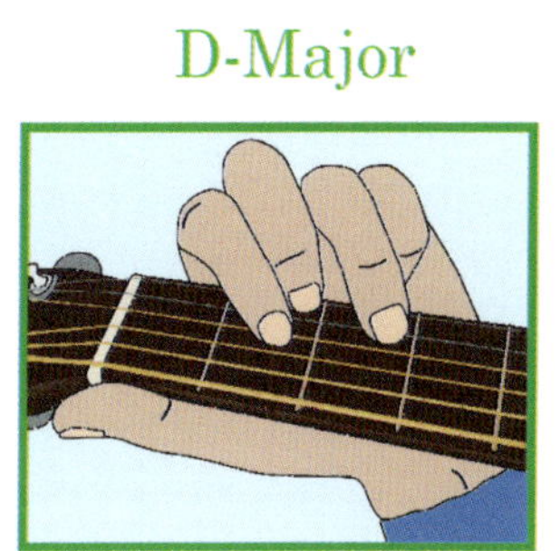

2x

A-Major

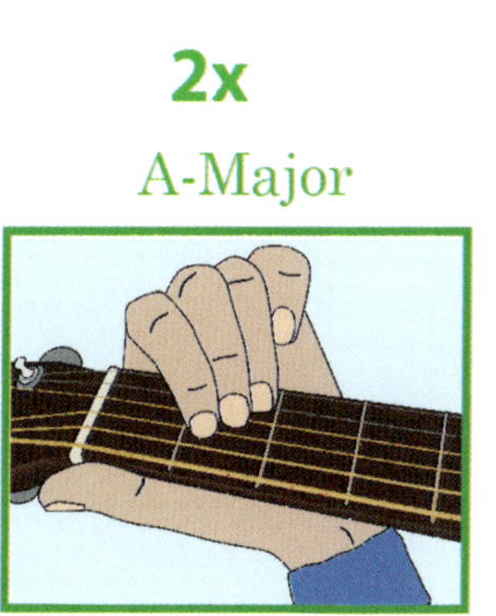

2x

E-Major

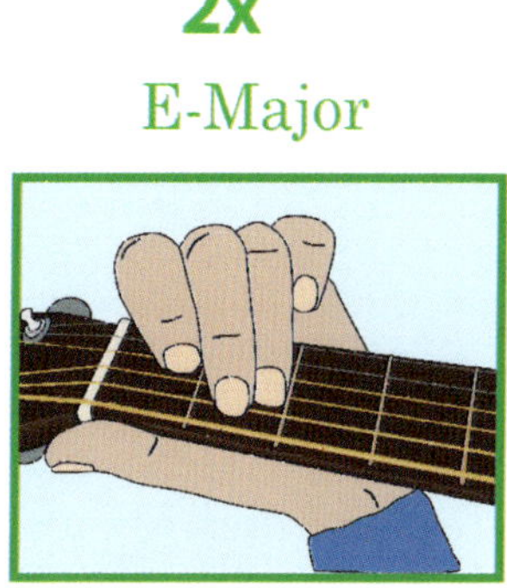

The wheels on the bus

Video

Measure: 2/4

Music: Traditional
Vocals: Traditional

Verse 1

A-Major A-Major
The Wheels on the bus go round and round,

E-Major A-Major
Round and round, round and round,

A-Major A-Major
The Wheels on the bus go round and round,

E-Major A-Major
All day long.

A-Major

Verse 2

A-Major A-Major
The wipers on the bus goes swish,swish swish,

E-Major A-Major
Swish swish swish, swish swish swish,

A-Major A-Major
The wipers on the bus goes swish, swish swish,

E-Major A-Major
All day long.

E-Major

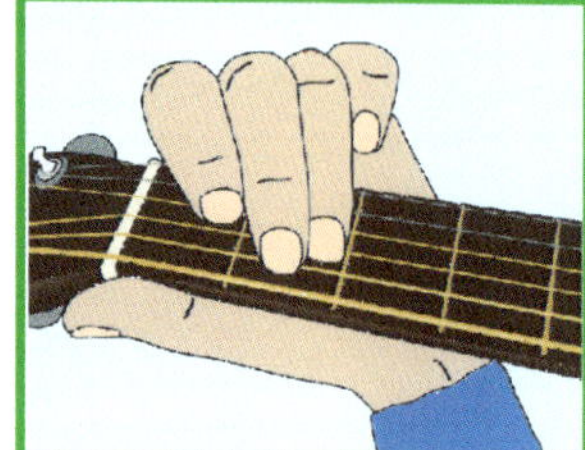

Playalong Song

Mary had a little lamb

Measure: 2/4

Music: Traditional
Vocals: Traditional

Verse 1

A-Major E-Major A-Major
Ma - ry had a lit - tle lamb, lit -tle lamb, lit -tle lamb,

A-Major E-Major A-Major
Ma - ry had a lit - tle lamb, it's fleece was white as snow,

A-Major E-Major A-Major
Eve - ry - where that Ma - ry went, Ma - ry went, Ma - ry went,

A-Major E-Major A-Major
Eve - ry - where that Ma - ry went, the lamb was sure to go.

Verse 2

A-Major E-Major A-Major
It fol - lowed her to school one day, school one day, school one day,

A-Major E-Major A-Major
It fol -lowed her to school one day , which was a - gainst the rules.

A-Major E-Major A-Major
It made the chil - dren laugh and play, laugh and play, laugh and play,

A-Major E-Major A-Major
It made the chil -dren laugh and play, to see a lamb at school.

Video Exercise   Playalong Song

8 Tips For Little Guitar Players

1) Make sure that your guitar is always tuned correctly. (Ask your parents for help if necessary).

2) Sit comfortably, but make sure that your guitar posture is on point, that will make playing a lot easier.

3) Slow down when playing new exercises and songs. You will automatically get faster once you know the exercise or song by heart.

4) Don't give up if something does not work out right away. You will be able to do it eventually, even if it takes 1, 2 or even 3 weeks in the beginning

5) Try playing your guitar several times per week. It helps to not store it away, but instead keep it handy in your room.

6) Listen to as much music as possible.

7) Show your parents whenever you have learned a new song or a new exercise.

8) Have fun playing the guitar and you will turn into an awesome guitarist.